THE STARTING POINT LIBRARY

INSECTS THAT LIVE TOGETHER

General Editors:

MICHAEL W. DEMPSEY AND ANGELA SHEEHAN

THE DANBURY PRESS

a division of Grolier Enterprises, Inc.

Published by the World Publishing Company.
© 1970 Macdonald and Company (Publishers) Ltd.
56789987

ant

Ants, termites, bees and wasps are all social insects. They are called social because they live together and help each other. Social means friendly and helpful.

termite

honeybee

Social insects live in colonies. The young insects stay with their parents all their lives. They live and work together somewhat in the way that people do. Each insect has its own special job.

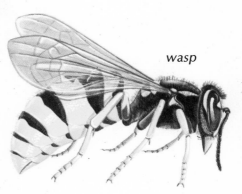

wasp

Most ants build their nests on the ground. These nests are called anthills.

Anthills are made of earth and dead leaves. Inside there are many rooms and tunnels.

This is a wood ants' nest.

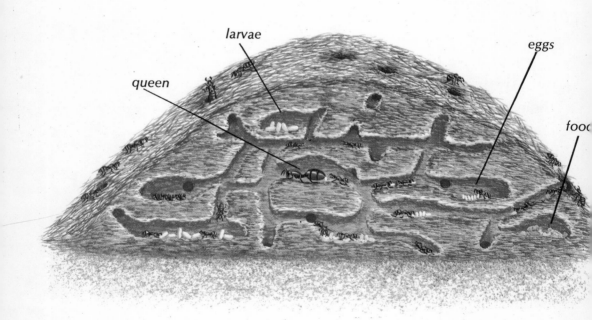

queen

larvae

eggs

food

Thousands of ants live in the nest.

Most of them are worker ants. The workers are females.

There are a few male ants, but they do not do any work.

The queen lays all the eggs.

When the queen is young, she has wings. Before she lays her eggs, her wings fall off and she grows very fat.

male

winged queen

worker

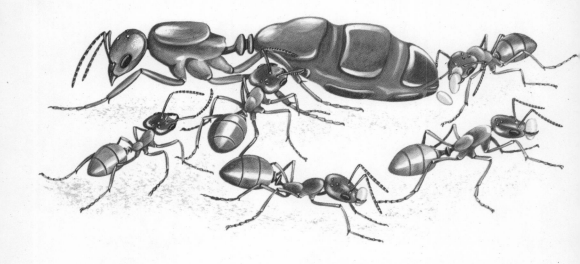

The worker ants look after the eggs and the young ants in the nest. When the queen lays her eggs, the workers take them to a special room where they will be safe and warm. They carry the eggs in their mouths. The eggs develop into ant babies called larvae.

If the nest is disturbed, the workers rush to hide the larvae and defend the young ants. Special big ants, called guards, make a circle around the nest. They fight the attackers.

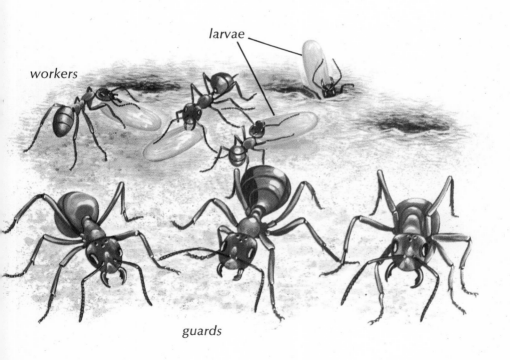

workers

larvae

guards

Ants help each other in many ways. These ants are carrying a leaf back to their nest. The leaf is much bigger than they are. They will use the leaf to repair holes in the nest.

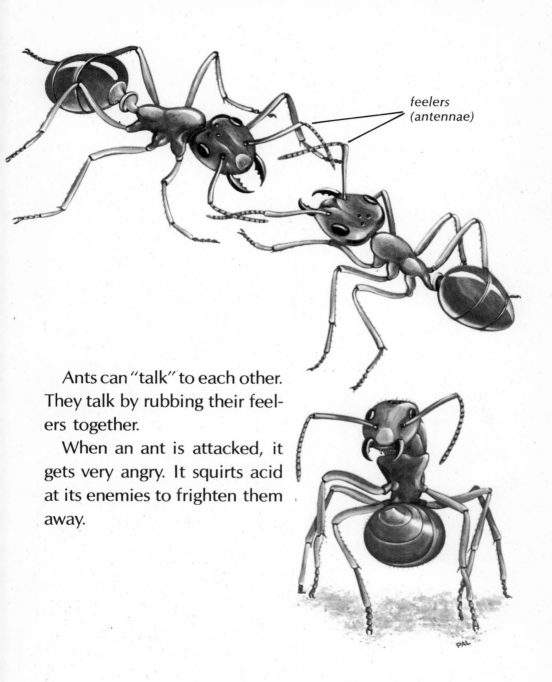

feelers
(antennae)

Ants can "talk" to each other.
They talk by rubbing their feelers together.

When an ant is attacked, it
gets very angry. It squirts acid
at its enemies to frighten them
away.

These are leafcutter ants. Leafcutter ants make their home in the ground. They cut up leaves with their strong jaws. They carry the leaves back to the nest. Underground, the leaves grow fungus. Ant larvae feed on the fungus.

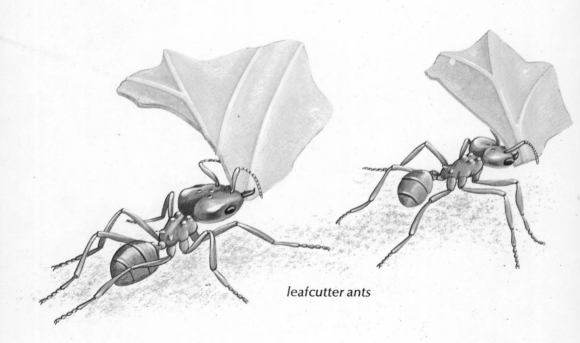

leafcutter ants

This is a honeycask ant. It is full of honey. The worker ants feed it, and it stores the food in its body. When the honey ants run short of food, their honey-cask has plenty to give them. Honey ants live only in dry lands.

honeycask ant

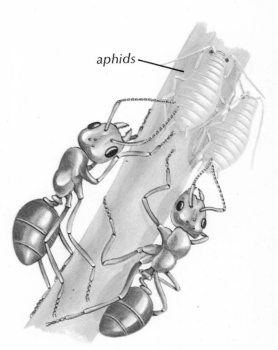

aphids

These ants are "milking" aphids. The ants get a kind of sweet juice from the aphids by stroking them. The sweet juice is called honeydew.

These are weaver ants. They live in Africa. Weaver ants make their nests from leaves. The young weaver ants make silk threads.

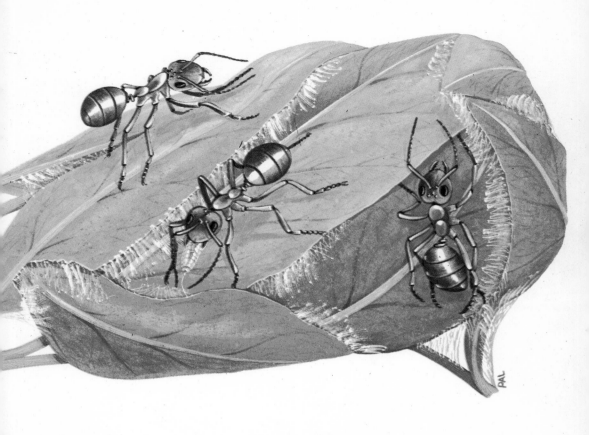

Workers use the silk to "sew" the leaves together. They sew with their mouths, instead of with needles. When the nest is finished, it is very safe and strong.

Army ants are found in the tropics. They do not build permanent nests. They move from place to place. They are called army ants because they look like soldiers marching.

When the army ants stop for a rest, the queen lays her eggs. The workers carry the eggs and the young ants in their mouths. As they march, the ants kill and eat any small animals which get in their way. Nothing seems to stop them. They often go through a house, and the people have to move out until the ants have gone.

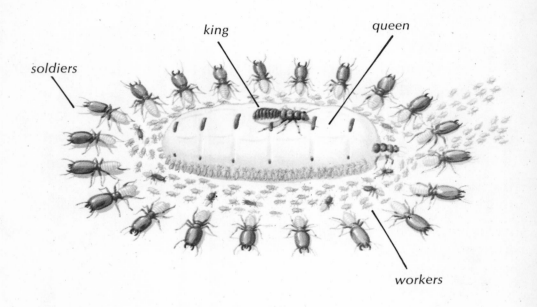

soldiers

king

queen

workers

Most kinds of termites are found in the tropics, but some live in other climates.

This is a colony of termites. The king and queen live in the middle of the nest. The queen lays millions of eggs. The eggs turn into workers and soldiers. The workers make the nest bigger and feed the young termites. The soldiers guard the nest.

Some termites make huge nests from mud. The nests are sometimes bigger than a man. There are millions of termites in such a nest.

Termites eat all kinds of wood. They are useful when they eat dead trees. They are harmful when they eat furniture and houses.

worker   queen   drone

These are honeybees. All three kinds are in each colony.
There is only one queen. She lays all the eggs.
There are many worker bees.
There are drones that do no work at all.
The honeybees' nest is called a hive. It contains thousands of cells. The cells are made of wax. They are called honeycombs.

pollen
"basket"

The workers collect food for the young bees in the nest. They collect sweet nectar from flowers and turn it into honey. They also collect pollen from the flowers. They put the pollen in "baskets" on their back legs.

When a worker finds some new flowers, it goes back to the hive to tell the others. It does a dance. The other workers can tell from the dance where the flowers are.

The cells in a comb are like rooms in a house. They are used for different purposes. Honey is stored in some cells and pollen is put in others. The queen lays her eggs in empty cells.

Young workers feed the queen and look after the grubs.

The queen sometimes lays over a thousand eggs in one day.

The eggs hatch into small white grubs. They all have to be fed. When the grubs have eaten enough food, workers cover the cells with wax.

Inside the cells the grubs change into pupa and then into young adults.

The fully grown bees eat their way through the wax covers. They are fed by workers until they are strong.

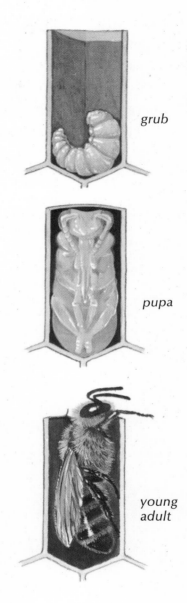

grub

pupa

young adult

When a colony becomes too large for the hive, it is time for another hive to be made. The queen leaves the nest, taking with her many of the worker bees and a few drones. They fly with her in a swarm.

The other workers stay behind in the nest with a newly-hatched queen.

A swarm of bees looks rather like a football.

When the swarm stops for a rest, a few scouts go to look for a place to build a new nest.

When they find a good place, the queen and her swarm fly off and start building a hive in the new location.

The honey that bees make is good to eat. People keep bees for their honey. The bees are kept in wooden hives that have removable combs.

The queen lays her eggs in cells at the bottom of the hive. The combs at the top are filled with honey by the worker bees.

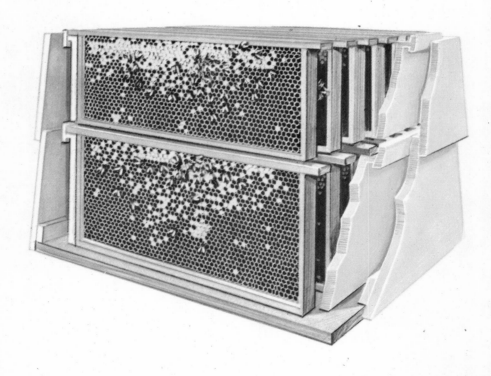

When the honeycombs are full, the beekeeper takes them from the hive.

He wears a special helmet so that the bees cannot sting him. He might puff smoke at the bees from a special kind of pipe. The smoke makes them too sleepy to sting.

In winter the bees cannot find much nectar, because there are not many flowers. The beekeeper feeds them sugar and water.

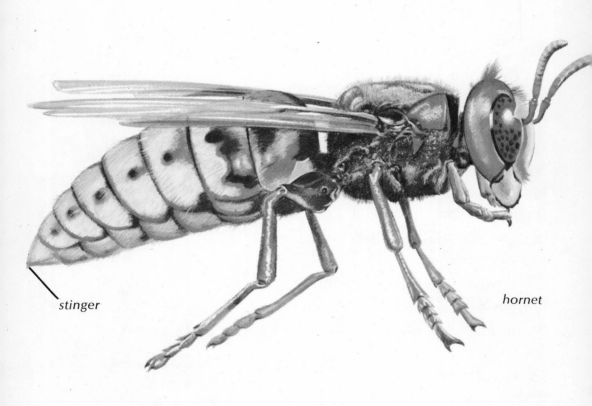

stinger

hornet

The hornet is a large wasp. Its sting is very painful.
Hornets feed on nectar, fruit juices and other insects.
They often build their nests on branches or in hollow trees.

The nest is made of hundreds of cells. The outside is covered with a paper-like material which the wasps make from chewed-up wood. There is an entrance at the bottom of the nest.

The hornet queen starts the nest and lays her eggs in the cells.

She feeds the young grubs with insects that workers have brought to the nest.

When they grow up, the new adults go outside to feed themselves. They also make the nest bigger.

outside
of nest

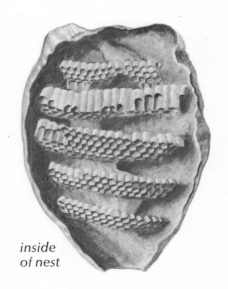

inside
of nest

There are many kinds of wasps other than the hornet. This is a paper wasp.

The queen wasp begins the nest. She builds some little cells and lays her eggs in them.

When the young wasps are ready to work, they build more cells so that the queen can lay more eggs.

A wasps' nest often has hundreds of cells.

cell

grub

paper cap

egg